2023 - 2027

Monhly Planner

Contact *Information*

Name :

Business :

Phone :

Email :

Website :

Name :

Business :

Phone :

Email :

Website :

Name :

Business :

Phone :

Email :

Website :

Name :

Business :

Phone :

Email :

Website :

Name :

Business :

Phone :

Email :

Website :

Name :

Business :

Phone :

Email :

Website :

Name :

Business :

Phone :

Email :

Website :

Name :

Business :

Phone :

Email :

Website :

Contact *Information*

Name :
Business :
Phone :
Email :
Website :

Name :
Business :
Phone :
Email :
Website :

Name :
Business :
Phone :
Email :
Website :

Name :
Business :
Phone :
Email :
Website :

Name :
Business :
Phone :
Email :
Website :

Name :
Business :
Phone :
Email :
Website :

Name :
Business :
Phone :
Email :
Website :

Name :
Business :
Phone :
Email :
Website :

Contact *Information*

Name :

Business :

Phone :

Email :

Website :

Name :

Business :

Phone :

Email :

Website :

Name :

Business :

Phone :

Email :

Website :

Name :

Business :

Phone :

Email :

Website :

Name :

Business :

Phone :

Email :

Website :

Name :

Business :

Phone :

Email :

Website :

Name :

Business :

Phone :

Email :

Website :

Name :

Business :

Phone :

Email :

Website :

Contact Information

Name :	Name :
Business :	Business :
Phone :	Phone :
Email :	Email :
Website :	Website :

Name :	Name :
Business :	Business :
Phone :	Phone :
Email :	Email :
Website :	Website :

Name :	Name :
Business :	Business :
Phone :	Phone :
Email :	Email :
Website :	Website :

Name :	Name :
Business :	Business :
Phone :	Phone :
Email :	Email :
Website :	Website :

2023 Calendar

January

S	M	T	W	T	F	S
1	2	3	4	5	6	7
8	9	10	11	12	13	14
15	16	17	18	19	20	21
22	23	24	25	26	27	28
29	30	31				

February

S	M	T	W	T	F	S
			1	2	3	4
5	6	7	8	9	10	11
12	13	14	15	16	17	18
19	20	21	22	23	24	25
26	27	28				

March

S	M	T	W	T	F	S
			1	2	3	4
5	6	7	8	9	10	11
12	13	14	15	16	17	18
19	20	21	22	23	24	25
26	27	28	29	30	31	

April

S	M	T	W	T	F	S
						1
2	3	4	5	6	7	8
9	10	11	12	13	14	15
16	17	18	19	20	21	22
23	24	25	26	27	28	29
30						

May

S	M	T	W	T	F	S
	1	2	3	4	5	6
7	8	9	10	11	12	13
14	15	16	17	18	19	20
21	22	23	24	25	26	27
28	29	30	31			

June

S	M	T	W	T	F	S
				1	2	3
4	5	6	7	8	9	10
11	12	13	14	15	16	17
18	19	20	21	22	23	24
25	26	27	28	29	30	

July

S	M	T	W	T	F	S
						1
2	3	4	5	6	7	8
9	10	11	12	13	14	15
16	17	18	19	20	21	22
23	24	25	26	27	28	29
30	31					

August

S	M	T	W	T	F	S
		1	2	3	4	5
6	7	8	9	10	11	12
13	14	15	16	17	18	19
20	21	22	23	24	25	26
27	28	29	30	31		

September

S	M	T	W	T	F	S
					1	2
3	4	5	6	7	8	9
10	11	12	13	14	15	16
17	18	19	20	21	22	23
24	25	26	27	28	29	30

October

S	M	T	W	T	F	S
1	2	3	4	5	6	7
8	9	10	11	12	13	14
15	16	17	18	19	20	21
22	23	24	25	26	27	28
29	30	31				

November

S	M	T	W	T	F	S
			1	2	3	4
5	6	7	8	9	10	11
12	13	14	15	16	17	18
19	20	21	22	23	24	25
26	27	28	29	30		

December

S	M	T	W	T	F	S
					1	2
3	4	5	6	7	8	9
10	11	12	13	14	15	16
17	18	19	20	21	22	23
24	25	26	27	28	29	30
31						

Notes

Notes

Monthly *Planner*

Month :

Monday

Tuesday

Wednesday

Thursday

Friday

Saturday

Sunday

Goals

Notes

Monthly *Planner*

Month :

Monday

Tuesday

Wednesday

Thursday

Friday

Saturday

Sunday

Goals

Notes

Monthly *Planner*

Month :

| Monday | | | | | |

| Tuesday | | | | | |

| Wednesday | | | | | |

| Thursday | | | | | |

| Friday | | | | | |

| Saturday | | | | | |

| Sunday | | | | | |

Goals

Notes

Monthly Planner

<table>
<tr><td>Month :</td></tr>
</table>

Monday				
Tuesday				
Wednesday				
Thursday				
Friday				
Saturday				
Sunday				

Goals

Notes

Monthly *Planner*

Monday				
Tuesday				
Wednesday				
Thursday				
Friday				
Saturday				
Sunday				

Goals

Notes

Monthly *Planner*

Month :

Monday

Tuesday

Wednesday

Thurday

Friday

Saturday

Sunday

Goals

Notes

Monthly Planner

Month :

Monday					

Tuesday					

Wednesday					

Thursday					

Friday					

Saturday					

Sunday					

Goals

Notes

Monthly *Planner*

Month :

Monday				

Tuesday				

Wednesday				

Thursday				

Friday				

Saturday				

Sunday				

Goals

Notes

Monthly *Planner*

Month :

<table>
<tr><td>Monday</td><td></td><td></td><td></td><td></td><td></td></tr>
<tr><td>Tuesday</td><td></td><td></td><td></td><td></td><td></td></tr>
<tr><td>Wednesday</td><td></td><td></td><td></td><td></td><td></td></tr>
<tr><td>Thursday</td><td></td><td></td><td></td><td></td><td></td></tr>
<tr><td>Friday</td><td></td><td></td><td></td><td></td><td></td></tr>
<tr><td>Saturday</td><td></td><td></td><td></td><td></td><td></td></tr>
<tr><td>Sunday</td><td></td><td></td><td></td><td></td><td></td></tr>
</table>

Goals

Notes

Monthly *Planner*

Monday

Tuesday

Wednesday

Thursday

Friday

Saturday

Sunday

Goals

Notes

Monthly *Planner*

Month :

<table>
<tr><td>Monday</td><td></td></tr>
<tr><td>Tuesday</td><td></td></tr>
<tr><td>Wednesday</td><td></td></tr>
<tr><td>Thursday</td><td></td></tr>
<tr><td>Friday</td><td></td></tr>
<tr><td>Saturday</td><td></td></tr>
<tr><td>Sunday</td><td></td></tr>
</table>

Goals

Notes

Monthly *Planner*

Month :

Monday

Tuesday

Wednesday

Thurday

Friday

Saturday

Sunday

Goals

Notes

2024 Calendar

January

S	M	T	W	T	F	S
	1	2	3	4	5	6
7	8	9	10	11	12	13
14	15	16	17	18	19	20
21	22	23	24	25	26	27
28	29	30	31			

February

S	M	T	W	T	F	S
				1	2	3
4	5	6	7	8	9	10
11	12	13	14	15	16	17
18	19	20	21	22	23	24
25	26	27	28	29		

March

S	M	T	W	T	F	S
					1	2
3	4	5	6	7	8	9
10	11	12	13	14	15	16
17	18	19	20	21	22	23
24 / 31	25	26	27	28	29	30

April

S	M	T	W	T	F	S
	1	2	3	4	5	6
7	8	9	10	11	12	13
14	15	16	17	18	19	20
21	22	23	24	25	26	27
28	29	30				

May

S	M	T	W	T	F	S
			1	2	3	4
5	6	7	8	9	10	11
12	13	14	15	16	17	18
19	20	21	22	23	24	25
26	27	28	29	30	31	

June

S	M	T	W	T	F	S
						1
2	3	4	5	6	7	8
9	10	11	12	13	14	15
16	17	18	19	20	21	22
23 / 30	24	25	26	27	28	29

July

S	M	T	W	T	F	S
	1	2	3	4	5	6
7	8	9	10	11	12	13
14	15	16	17	18	19	20
21	22	23	24	25	26	27
28	29	30	31			

August

S	M	T	W	T	F	S
				1	2	3
4	5	6	7	8	9	10
11	12	13	14	15	16	17
18	19	20	21	22	23	24
25	26	27	28	29	30	31

September

S	M	T	W	T	F	S
1	2	3	4	5	6	7
8	9	10	11	12	13	14
15	16	17	18	19	20	21
22	23	24	25	26	27	28
29	30					

October

S	M	T	W	T	F	S
		1	2	3	4	5
6	7	8	9	10	11	12
13	14	15	16	17	18	19
20	21	22	23	24	25	26
27	28	29	30	31		

November

S	M	T	W	T	F	S
					1	2
3	4	5	6	7	8	9
10	11	12	13	14	15	16
17	18	19	20	21	22	23
24	25	26	27	28	29	30

December

S	M	T	W	T	F	S
1	2	3	4	5	6	7
8	9	10	11	12	13	14
15	16	17	18	19	20	21
22	23	24	25	26	27	28
29	30	31				

Notes

Notes

Monthly *Planner*

Month :

Monday				
Tuesday				
Wednesday				
Thursday				
Friday				
Saturday				
Sunday				

Goals

Notes

Monthly *Planner*

Month :

| Monday | | | | |

| Tuesday | | | | |

| Wednesday | | | | |

| Thursday | | | | |

| Friday | | | | |

| Saturday | | | | |

| Sunday | | | | |

Goals

Notes

Monthly *Planner*

Month :

	Monday
	Tuesday
	Wednesday
	Thurday
	Friday
	Saturday
	Sunday

Monthly *Planner*

Month :

Monday					

Tuesday					

Wednesday					

Thursday					

Friday					

Saturday					

Sunday					

Goals

Notes

Monthly *Planner*

Month :

Monday				

Tuesday				

Wednesday				

Thurday				

Friday				

Saturday				

Sunday				

Goals

Notes

Monthly *Planner*

Monthly *Planner*

Month :

Monday				

Tuesday				

Wednesday				

Thursday				

Friday				

Saturday				

Sunday				

Goals

Notes

Monthly *Planner*

Month :

Monday

Tuesday

Wednesday

Thursday

Notes

Friday

Saturday

Sunday

Monthly *Planner*

Month :

Monday
Tuesday
Wednesday
Thurday
Friday
Saturday
Sunday

Goals

Notes

Monthly Planner

Month :

Monday				
Tuesday				
Wednesday				
Thursday				
Friday				
Saturday				
Sunday				

Goals

Notes

Monthly *Planner*

Month :

<table>
<tr><td rowspan="1">Monday</td><td></td><td></td><td></td><td></td><td></td></tr>
<tr><td>Tuesday</td><td></td><td></td><td></td><td></td><td></td></tr>
<tr><td>Wednesday</td><td></td><td></td><td></td><td></td><td></td></tr>
<tr><td>Thurday</td><td></td><td></td><td></td><td></td><td></td></tr>
<tr><td>Friday</td><td></td><td></td><td></td><td></td><td></td></tr>
<tr><td>Saturday</td><td></td><td></td><td></td><td></td><td></td></tr>
<tr><td>Sunday</td><td></td><td></td><td></td><td></td><td></td></tr>
</table>

Goals

Notes

Monthly *Planner*

Month :

Monday

Tuesday

Wednesday

Thursday

Friday

Saturday

Sunday

Goals

Notes

2025 Calendar

January

S	M	T	W	T	F	S
			1	2	3	4
5	6	7	8	9	10	11
12	13	14	15	16	17	18
19	20	21	22	23	24	25
26	27	28	29	30	31	

February

S	M	T	W	T	F	S
						1
2	3	4	5	6	7	8
9	10	11	12	13	14	15
16	17	18	19	20	21	22
23	24	25	26	27	28	

March

S	M	T	W	T	F	S
						1
2	3	4	5	6	7	8
9	10	11	12	13	14	15
16	17	18	19	20	21	22
23	24	25	26	27	28	29
30	31					

April

S	M	T	W	T	F	S
		1	2	3	4	5
6	7	8	9	10	11	12
13	14	15	16	17	18	19
20	21	22	23	24	25	26
27	28	29	30			

May

S	M	T	W	T	F	S
				1	2	3
4	5	6	7	8	9	10
11	12	13	14	15	16	17
18	19	20	21	22	23	24
25	26	27	28	29	30	31

June

S	M	T	W	T	F	S
1	2	3	4	5	6	7
8	9	10	11	12	13	14
15	16	17	18	19	20	21
22	23	24	25	26	27	28
29	30					

July

S	M	T	W	T	F	S
		1	2	3	4	5
6	7	8	9	10	11	12
13	14	15	16	17	18	19
20	21	22	23	24	25	26
27	28	29	30	31		

August

S	M	T	W	T	F	S
					1	2
3	4	5	6	7	8	9
10	11	12	13	14	15	16
17	18	19	20	21	22	23
24	25	26	27	28	29	30
31						

September

S	M	T	W	T	F	S
	1	2	3	4	5	6
7	8	9	10	11	12	13
14	15	16	17	18	19	20
21	22	23	24	25	26	27
28	29	30				

October

S	M	T	W	T	F	S
		1	2	3	4	
5	6	7	8	9	10	11
12	13	14	15	16	17	18
19	20	21	22	23	24	25
26	27	28	29	30	31	

November

S	M	T	W	T	F	S
						1
2	3	4	5	6	7	8
9	10	11	12	13	14	15
16	17	18	19	20	21	22
23	24	25	26	27	28	29
30						

December

S	M	T	W	T	F	S
	1	2	3	4	5	6
7	8	9	10	11	12	13
14	15	16	17	18	19	20
21	22	23	24	25	26	27
28	29	30	31			

Notes

Notes

Monthly *Planner*

Month :

Monthly *Planner*

Monday

Tuesday

Wednesday

Thursday

Friday

Saturday

Sunday

Goals

Notes

Monthly *Planner*

Month :

Monday				

Tuesday				

Wednesday				

Thurday				

Friday				

Saturday				

Sunday				

Goals

Notes

Monthly *Planner*

Month :

Monday				

Tuesday				

Wednesday				

Thursday				

Friday				

Saturday				

Sunday				

Goals

Notes

Monthly Planner

Month :

	Monday				

Goals

| | Tuesday | | | | |

| | Wednesday | | | | |

Notes

| | Thursday | | | | |

| | Friday | | | | |

| | Saturday | | | | |

| | Sunday | | | | |

Monthly *Planner*

Month :

| Monday |
| Tuesday |
| Wednesday |
| Thursday |
| Friday |
| Saturday |
| Sunday |

Monthly *Planner*

Month :

<table>
<tr><td>Monday</td><td></td><td></td><td></td><td></td><td></td></tr>
<tr><td>Tuesday</td><td></td><td></td><td></td><td></td><td></td></tr>
<tr><td>Wednesday</td><td></td><td></td><td></td><td></td><td></td></tr>
<tr><td>Thursday</td><td></td><td></td><td></td><td></td><td></td></tr>
<tr><td>Friday</td><td></td><td></td><td></td><td></td><td></td></tr>
<tr><td>Saturday</td><td></td><td></td><td></td><td></td><td></td></tr>
<tr><td>Sunday</td><td></td><td></td><td></td><td></td><td></td></tr>
</table>

Goals

Notes

Monthly *Planner*

Month :

Monday				
Tuesday				
Wednesday				
Thursday				
Friday				
Saturday				
Sunday				

Goals

Notes

Monthly *Planner*

Month :

<table>
<tr><td>Monday</td><td></td><td></td><td></td><td></td><td></td></tr>
<tr><td>Tuesday</td><td></td><td></td><td></td><td></td><td></td></tr>
<tr><td>Wednesday</td><td></td><td></td><td></td><td></td><td></td></tr>
<tr><td>Thursday</td><td></td><td></td><td></td><td></td><td></td></tr>
<tr><td>Friday</td><td></td><td></td><td></td><td></td><td></td></tr>
<tr><td>Saturday</td><td></td><td></td><td></td><td></td><td></td></tr>
<tr><td>Sunday</td><td></td><td></td><td></td><td></td><td></td></tr>
</table>

Goals

Notes

Monthly *Planner*

Month :

Monday				
Tuesday				
Wednesday				
Thursday				
Friday				
Saturday				
Sunday				

Goals

Notes

Monthly *Planner*

Month :

Monday				
Tuesday				
Wednesday				
Thursday				
Friday				
Saturday				
Sunday				

Goals

Notes

Monthly *Planner*

Month :

<table>
<tr><td>Monday</td><td></td><td></td><td></td><td></td><td></td></tr>
<tr><td>Tuesday</td><td></td><td></td><td></td><td></td><td></td></tr>
<tr><td>Wednesday</td><td></td><td></td><td></td><td></td><td></td></tr>
<tr><td>Thurday</td><td></td><td></td><td></td><td></td><td></td></tr>
<tr><td>Friday</td><td></td><td></td><td></td><td></td><td></td></tr>
<tr><td>Saturday</td><td></td><td></td><td></td><td></td><td></td></tr>
<tr><td>Sunday</td><td></td><td></td><td></td><td></td><td></td></tr>
</table>

Goals

Notes

2026 Calendar

January

S	M	T	W	T	F	S
				1	2	3
4	5	6	7	8	9	10
11	12	13	14	15	16	17
18	19	20	21	22	23	24
25	26	27	28	29	30	31

February

S	M	T	W	T	F	S
1	2	3	4	5	6	7
8	9	10	11	12	13	14
15	16	17	18	19	20	21
22	23	24	25	26	27	28

March

S	M	T	W	T	F	S
1	2	3	4	5	6	7
8	9	10	11	12	13	14
15	16	17	18	19	20	21
22	23	24	25	26	27	28
29	30	31				

April

S	M	T	W	T	F	S
			1	2	3	4
5	6	7	8	9	10	11
12	13	14	15	16	17	18
19	20	21	22	23	24	25
26	27	28	29	30		

May

S	M	T	W	T	F	S
					1	2
3	4	5	6	7	8	9
10	11	12	13	14	15	16
17	18	19	20	21	22	23
24	25	26	27	28	29	30
31						

June

S	M	T	W	T	F	S
	1	2	3	4	5	6
7	8	9	10	11	12	13
14	15	16	17	18	19	20
21	22	23	24	25	26	27
28	29	30				

July

S	M	T	W	T	F	S
			1	2	3	4
5	6	7	8	9	10	11
12	13	14	15	16	17	18
19	20	21	22	23	24	25
26	27	28	29	30	31	

August

S	M	T	W	T	F	S
						1
2	3	4	5	6	7	8
9	10	11	12	13	14	15
16	17	18	19	20	21	22
23	24	25	26	27	28	29
30	31					

September

S	M	T	W	T	F	S
		1	2	3	4	5
6	7	8	9	10	11	12
13	14	15	16	17	18	19
20	21	22	23	24	25	26
27	28	29	30			

October

S	M	T	W	T	F	S
				1	2	3
4	5	6	7	8	9	10
11	12	13	14	15	16	17
18	19	20	21	22	23	24
25	26	27	28	29	30	31

November

S	M	T	W	T	F	S
1	2	3	4	5	6	7
8	9	10	11	12	13	14
15	16	17	18	19	20	21
22	23	24	25	26	27	28
29	30					

December

S	M	T	W	T	F	S
		1	2	3	4	5
6	7	8	9	10	11	12
13	14	15	16	17	18	19
20	21	22	23	24	25	26
27	28	29	30	31		

Notes

Notes

Monthly *Planner*

Month :

	Goals

Monday

Tuesday

Wednesday

Thursday

Friday

Saturday

Sunday

Notes

Monthly *Planner*

Month :

Monday					

Tuesday					

Wednesday					

Thursday					

Friday					

Saturday					

Sunday					

Goals

Notes

Monthly *Planner*

Month :

Monday					

Tuesday					

Wednesday					

Thursday					

Friday					

Saturday					

Sunday					

Goals

Notes

Monthly *Planner*

Month :

Monday					

Tuesday					

Wednesday					

Thursday					

Friday					

Saturday					

Sunday					

Goals

Notes

Monthly *Planner*

Month :

| Monday |
| Tuesday |
| Wednesday |
| Thurday |
| Friday |
| Saturday |
| Sunday |

Goals

Notes

Monthly *Planner*

Month :

| Monday | | | | | |

| Tuesday | | | | | |

| Wednesday | | | | | |

| Thursday | | | | | |

| Friday | | | | | |

| Saturday | | | | | |

| Sunday | | | | | |

Goals

Notes

Monthly *Planner*

Month :

Monday				
Tuesday				
Wednesday				
Thursday				
Friday				
Saturday				
Sunday				

Goals

Notes

Monthly *Planner*

Month :

Monday					

Tuesday					

Wednesday					

Thursday					

Friday					

Saturday					

Sunday					

Goals

Notes

Monthly *Planner*

Month :

Monday

Tuesday

Wednesday

Thursday

Friday

Saturday

Sunday

Goals

Notes

Monthly *Planner*

Month :

Monday					

Tuesday					

Wednesday					

Thursday					

Friday					

Saturday					

Sunday					

Goals

Notes

Monthly *Planner*

Month :

Monday				

Tuesday				

Wednesday				

Thursday				

Friday				

Saturday				

Sunday				

Goals

Notes

Monthly *Planner*

Month :

Monday				
Tuesday				
Wednesday				
Thursday				
Friday				
Saturday				
Sunday				

Goals

Notes

2027 Calendar

January

S	M	T	W	T	F	S
					1	2
3	4	5	6	7	8	9
10	11	12	13	14	15	16
17	18	19	20	21	22	23
24 31	25	26	27	28	29	30

February

S	M	T	W	T	F	S
	1	2	3	4	5	6
7	8	9	10	11	12	13
14	15	16	17	18	19	20
21	22	23	24	25	26	27
28						

March

S	M	T	W	T	F	S
	1	2	3	4	5	6
7	8	9	10	11	12	13
14	15	16	17	18	19	20
21	22	23	24	25	26	27
28	29	30	31			

April

S	M	T	W	T	F	S
				1	2	3
4	5	6	7	8	9	10
11	12	13	14	15	16	17
18	19	20	21	22	23	24
25	26	27	28	29	30	

May

S	M	T	W	T	F	S
						1
2	3	4	5	6	7	8
9	10	11	12	13	14	15
16	17	18	19	20	21	22
23 30	24 31	25	26	27	28	29

June

S	M	T	W	T	F	S
		1	2	3	4	5
6	7	8	9	10	11	12
13	14	15	16	17	18	19
20	21	22	23	24	25	26
27	28	29	30			

July

S	M	T	W	T	F	S
				1	2	3
4	5	6	7	8	9	10
11	12	13	14	15	16	17
18	19	20	21	22	23	24
25	26	27	28	29	30	31

August

S	M	T	W	T	F	S
1	2	3	4	5	6	7
8	9	10	11	12	13	14
15	16	17	18	19	20	21
22	23	24	25	26	27	28
29	30	31				

September

S	M	T	W	T	F	S
			1	2	3	4
5	6	7	8	9	10	11
12	13	14	15	16	17	18
19	20	21	22	23	24	25
26	27	28	29	30		

October

S	M	T	W	T	F	S
					1	2
3	4	5	6	7	8	9
10	11	12	13	14	15	16
17	18	19	20	21	22	23
24	25	26	27	28	29	30
31						

November

S	M	T	W	T	F	S
	1	2	3	4	5	6
7	8	9	10	11	12	13
14	15	16	17	18	19	20
21	22	23	24	25	26	27
28	29	30				

December

S	M	T	W	T	F	S
			1	2	3	4
5	6	7	8	9	10	11
12	13	14	15	16	17	18
19	20	21	22	23	24	25
26	27	28	29	30	31	

Notes

Notes

Monthly *Planner*

Month :

Monday

Tuesday

Wednesday

Thursday

Friday

Saturday

Sunday

Goals

Notes

Monthly *Planner*

Month :

Monday

Tuesday

Wednesday

Thurday

Friday

Saturday

Sunday

Goals

Notes

Monthly *Planner*

Month :

Monday

Tuesday

Wednesday

Thursday

Friday

Saturday

Sunday

Goals

Notes

Monthly *Planner*

Month :

Monday					

Tuesday					

Wednesday					

Thursday					

Friday					

Saturday					

Sunday					

Goals

Notes

Monthly *Planner*

Month :

Goals

Notes

Monday

Tuesday

Wednesday

Thursday

Friday

Saturday

Sunday

Monthly *Planner*

Month :

Monday				

Tuesday				

Wednesday				

Thurday				

Friday				

Saturday				

Sunday				

Goals

Notes

Monthly *Planner*

Month :

Monday					

Tuesday					

Wednesday					

Thursday					

Friday					

Saturday					

Sunday					

Goals

Notes

Monthly *Planner*

Month :

<table>
<tr><td>Monday</td><td></td><td></td><td></td><td></td><td></td></tr>
<tr><td>Tuesday</td><td></td><td></td><td></td><td></td><td></td></tr>
<tr><td>Wednesday</td><td></td><td></td><td></td><td></td><td></td></tr>
<tr><td>Thursday</td><td></td><td></td><td></td><td></td><td></td></tr>
<tr><td>Friday</td><td></td><td></td><td></td><td></td><td></td></tr>
<tr><td>Saturday</td><td></td><td></td><td></td><td></td><td></td></tr>
<tr><td>Sunday</td><td></td><td></td><td></td><td></td><td></td></tr>
</table>

Goals

Notes

Monthly *Planner*

Month :

Monthly *Planner*

Month :

Goals

Notes

Monthly *Planner*

Month :

	Goals

Monday

Tuesday

Wednesday

Thursday

Friday

Saturday

Sunday

Notes

Monthly *Planner*

Month :

Monday

Tuesday

Wednesday

Thursday

Friday

Saturday

Sunday

Goals

Notes

Notes

Notes

Notes

Notes

Notes

Notes

Notes

Notes

Notes